Carolyn Jones

Adventures with Tony and Lou

Ernst Klett Verlag
Stuttgart · Leipzig

Contents

Before you read the story

1 All about adventures

a) *An adventure is an activity that you do that is very exciting. Maybe it's also something new for you. Where can you have adventures? Look at the kite's* (Drachen) *tails for eight ideas, and write them down on a piece of paper. There is one example for you.*

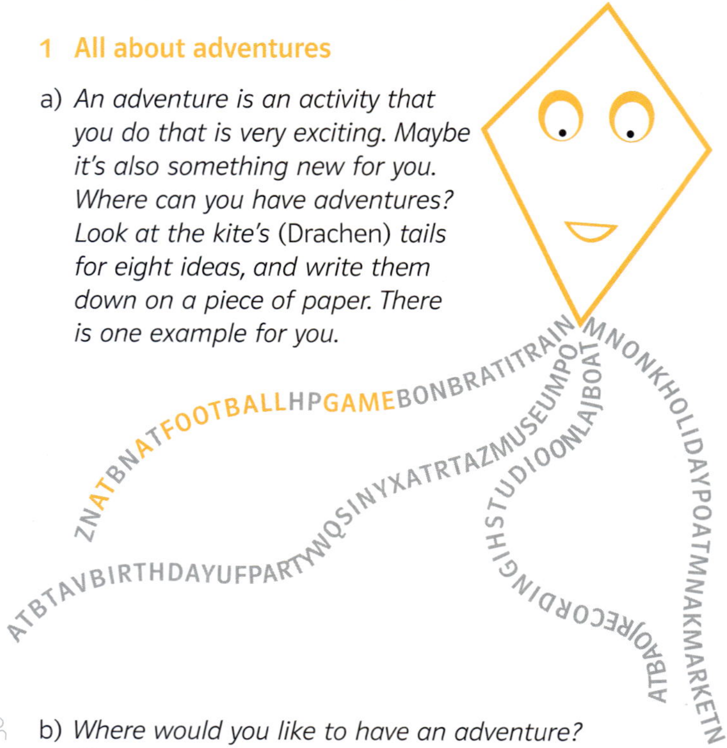

b) *Where would you like to have an adventure? Choose one of the places from a). Tell your partner why, and listen to his/her idea.*

c) *Where else can you have an adventure? Or what else can you do?*

2 Tony and Lou's adventures

a) *Look at the cover. Tony and Lou are having an adventure when they fly* (fliegen) *with a bird* (Vogel)*. How do you think Tony, Lou and the bird feel? Why do you think Tony and Lou are on a bird's back?*

b) *What other adventures would you like Tony and Lou to have?*

A birthday to remember

Tony wakes up early, like every morning when the children come into Thomas Tallis School. They are laughing and talking and it's very loud in the mouse hole under the stairs. But today Tony is feeling very happy and excited. "*Happy Birthday to me! Happy Birthday to me! Happy Birthday, dear Tony! Happy Birthday to me!*" he sings.

"Oh yes. Thanks for reminding me!" says Lou and laughs. "Happy Birthday, Tony! Look – I've got a card and a present for you!"

"Wow, thank you!" says Tony.

He jumps out of bed and takes the present from Lou. 'What is it?' he thinks. 'Lou knows I *really* want a kite, but this is a little small.' He unwraps it quickly. It's a T-shirt with a big picture of a kite on it.

"Oh, thanks, Lou," he says.

"You're welcome!" says Lou. "I hope it's the right size."

"It's ... er ... great," says Tony, but he feels a little disappointed.

'A T-shirt with a picture of a kite isn't the same as a *real* one,' he thinks. But he puts on his new T-shirt, sits at the table and starts writing a long list.

"What are you doing?" asks Lou.

"I still have so much to do for my birthday party! Everyone is coming this afternoon!" Tony answers.

Lou is very quiet. She's got a problem. Tony can't stop talking about his birthday party – the one that *he's* planning.

What he doesn't know is that Lou and his friends are already planning a surprise birthday party for him.

---

1 **to wake up** [weɪk‿ˈʌp] aufwachen • 3 **mouse hole** [ˈmaʊs həʊl] Mauseloch • 4 **stairs** *(pl)* [steəz] Treppe • 8 **to remind sb** [rɪˈmaɪnd] jmdn. erinnern • 13 **kite** [kaɪt] Drachen • 20 **real** [rɪəl] echt

"I need to go to the Art room for decorations and to the kitchen for more food," Tony says. "And ... oh no! I need to talk to DJ Music Mouse about the music!"

"But look at this place!" says Lou. "Our mouse hole is a mess and we can't have a party here when it looks like this!"

Tony looks around. "I guess you're right," he says.

Lou thinks quickly. "I have an idea," she says. "You stay here and clean and tidy and I'll go school shopping." That's what the mice call it when they use things from Thomas Tallis School.

"OK," Tony says. "But *then* I need to go and find DJ Music Mouse."

"Ernie wants to go with you and help you choose the music," says Lou. "Please wait for him. So you have enough time to clean."

"Great," says Tony, but he doesn't sound very happy.

5 mess [mes] Durcheinander, Unordnung • **9 I'll** [aɪl] Ich werde

Lou runs out of their mouse hole, through a tunnel to the Art room. There are no children in there now, so she can meet her friend here.

"Ernie!" says Lou. "You *must* go and see Tony. He's waiting for you at home. "He thinks that you want to go with him to DJ Music Mouse and talk about the music for his party. Please don't let him come here to the Art room or to the kitchen for food or decorations! We need them for *our* party!"

"Of course I'll go with him. But I've got a *big* problem too," says Ernie. "It's about Tony's kite." He shows Lou the kite. My friend put the name *Tom*, not *Tony*, on it. We can't give it to him like that!"

"Oh no!" says Lou. "We must think of something fast."

Lou thinks for a moment, then says "I have an idea! Do you see those paints and paint brushes on the tables? Let's use them to change the word *Tom* into *Tony*!"

"Cool!" says Ernie. "But we must do it later. There's another class coming in five minutes! Let's wait for the next break."

"Ok," says Lou as she and Ernie run out of the classroom.

• • •

Lou knocks on Blossom's door.

"Come in, come in!" says Blossom. "I'm so happy you're here, Lou!"

"Come and see Tony's cake!" says Blossom. She takes Lou's hand and pulls her into the kitchen.

"Wow! That's a really cool cake!" says Lou. "And so many decorations! Tony loves cheesecake!"

---

16 **paint** [peɪnt] Farbe • 16 **paint brush** [ˈpeɪnt ˌbrʌʃ] Pinsel • 17 **to change** [tʃeɪndʒ] ändern • 23 **to knock** [nɒk] klopfen

"*Cheese*cake?" says Blossom. "No, it isn't a cheesecake, it's a *sponge* cake. That's OK, isn't it?"

Lou doesn't know what to say. "I'm sorry, Blossom, but he doesn't like sponge cake at all! We can't give him this one. Oh dear … now we've got *another* problem!"

Blossom is very disappointed and they are thinking about what they can do when suddenly the door opens and Gus runs into Blossom's kitchen.

"Lou, Blossom, I've got a *big* problem!" Gus shouts. 'Oh no! Not *another* problem!' thinks Lou. "What's wrong, Gus?" she asks.

"We can't have the party at my place! Water from the Science room came in through my ceiling last night. There's water everywhere. We must move the party to another mouse hole. It's awful!"

"I think we need a meeting," says Lou. "Let's go and tell everyone that they must come here to Blossom's house in ten minutes."

• • •

Ernie gets to Tony's house. "Happy Birthday, Tony!" he says.

"Hello, hello!" says Tony. "I'm so happy to see you! I don't like tidying the place, but I must for my party! Can you please help me? Then we can go and talk to DJ Music Mouse!"

"Sure, Tony," says Ernie and laughs. "When it's not one but two mice, even cleaning can be nice!"

• • •

10 **What's wrong?** [wɒts ˈrɒŋ] Was ist los? • 13 **science** [ˈsaɪəns] *hier:* Naturwissenschaften • 13 **came** [keɪm] kam • 13 **ceiling** [ˈsiːlɪŋ] Zimmerdecke • 16 **meeting** [ˈmiːtɪŋ] Besprechung, Versammlung

Ten minutes later, Lou, Gus and and all their friends are in Blossom's kitchen. "Have some sponge cake!" says Blossom as she puts a big piece on everyone's plate. Tony doesn't like it so we can eat it all!"

"Don't worry! *We* like it!" says Gus.

"Right," says Lou. "Quiet everyone. We must talk about this afternoon. There are three problems: a kite with the wrong name, the wrong cake and the water in Gus's house."

"We can have a swimming party!" says somebody.

"Very funny!" says Lou. "I think we can change the name on the kite in the Art room …"

"… and I can try to make a cheesecake," says Blossom. "I just hope that the right cheese is in the school kitchen."

"OK, now we've only got the *big* problem left. Where can we have the party? Any ideas?"

Everyone talks at the same time. "My house is too small." "My neighbours don't like loud music and dancing". Finally, Blossom says, "OK, we can have the party here. My house isn't very big, but we can use the school garden too. I can put milk in the hall to keep the cat away. Can you all come here at three o'clock with your costumes?"

"Sure!" says Lou. "Now Gus and I must run to the Art room, change the name on Tony's kite and get some paper for the decorations. You can all help make them when Gus and I get back."

• • •

"OK," says Lou to Gus in the Art room. "Let's put the kite on the table and use this blue paint. We must try and change the letter '*m*' in Tom to '*ny*' for *Tony*."

3 plate [pleɪt] Teller • **21 hall** [hɔːl] Flur

They try to hold the paint brush together, but it's too big.

"Oh no, we can't do this!" says Gus. "Now what?"

"Hmmm … I know! I can use my tail!" Lou puts her tail in blue paint, then she paints over the letters. The kite looks great and they are happy.

"Now let's take lots of coloured paper for the decorations and get back to Blossom's house," says Lou.

Just then, the Art teacher opens the door. She screams when she sees the mice and runs away.

"It's lucky that she's scared of us." says Gus. "It gives us more time to find paper for the decorations."

7 **coloured** ['kʌləd] farbig, bunt • 9 **to scream** [skriːm] schreien

Tony and Ernie are back at Tony and Lou's mouse hole. Now DJ Music Mouse knows what music to play.

"Thanks for your help with the music list, Ernie," says Tony. "And thanks for helping me to tidy and clean our place! My party is going to be so great! I love parties!"

Suddenly, Gus runs into Tony's house.

"Hey Tony! Happy Birthday! Look! I have a message from Lou." Tony reads the note:

Tony, can you come to Blossom's house for tea at four o'clock? She doesn't feel good, so she can't come to your party, but she wants to see you on your birthday. Lou

'Four o'clock? My friends are supposed to come here then!' thinks Tony. But Blossom is also his friend and he knows that his other friends will understand if he's late.

• • •

At four o'clock Tony gets to Blossom's house. He knocks on the door. "Lou? Blossom?" he calls, but there is no answer. He knocks again. Everything is very quiet.

'I don't understand,' he thinks. 'Something's wrong.' He looks back again at Blossom's door and now he can hear voices. Somebody is whispering and laughing. What's happening? He knocks on the door again, and this time, when the door opens, two cats run out – with an alien, a monster, a rabbit and a sailor!

"*Surprise*!" they all shout, and everyone starts singing "Happy Birthday to you!" Tony can't believe it.

"Do you like our costumes?" they shout. "Look, here are your pilot goggles. You're a pilot for the day!" Tony can't speak – a pilot? Does this mean …?

12 **to be supposed to** [biː ˌsəˈpəʊzd] sollen • 13 **also** [ˈɔːlsəʊ] auch • 14 **will understand** [wɪl‿ʌndəˈstænd] werden verstehen • 27 **pilot** [ˈpaɪlət] Pilot • 27 **goggles** *(pl)* [ˈɡɒɡls] Schutzbrille • 28 **to mean** [miːn] *hier:* bedeuten

"Here's your present," says Lou. "Come on, open it!" Tony takes off the wrapping paper – and sees the kite of his dreams in front of his eyes!

"Happy Birthday, Tony!" says Blossom as she comes outside. "I've got a very special cheesecake for you!"

Tony feels very lucky. He's got some very good friends. How did Lou do it? He didn't know a thing! What a surprise! And now everyone is dancing and singing and Tony is eating his third piece of cheesecake. 'This is *really* a birthday to remember!' he thinks.

2 **wrapping paper** [ˈræpɪŋ ˌpeɪpə] Geschenkpapier • 3 **dream** [driːm] Traum • 3 **eye** [aɪ] Auge

Up, up and away

Tony wakes up, jumps out of bed and goes to the kitchen to make breakfast. Lou is already there.

“Let’s see if we can go outside today,” he says and opens the door to the schoolyard. He and Lou look outside their mouse hole. It’s sunny and just a little windy.

“It’s a great day to fly your kite!” says Lou. “And I want to ride my bike, but … it isn’t here!” she says.

Tony looks again. “How is that possible?” he asks.

“I don’t know. I always put it outside the door.”

“Ha! That’s why I always tell you to bring it inside!” says Tony. “But that’s very strange.”

“Maybe one of our friends is using it,” Lou says.

“Let’s call everyone to come and see me fly my kite and we can ask them about your bike too,” Tony says.

They are so excited about the kite and the bike that they don’t think about breakfast any more. Lou runs through all the tunnels under the school and shouts, “Come out into the yard! Tony is flying his kite. And who knows where my bike is?”

Ernie is excited to see the kite again and runs over. He wants to show Tony how it’s best to hold it.

“Like this, like this …” Ernie says, but Tony isn’t listening. He doesn’t need Ernie to tell him how to fly it.

Suddenly the kite flies up, and everyone claps.

“Wow,” says Tony, “this is so cool …” and just at that moment a gust of wind blows and suddenly his feet aren’t on the ground any more! The wind takes him up into a tree.

up [ʌp] aufwärts, hinauf • 4 **(school)yard** [ˈsku:l ˌjɑ:d] (Schul)hof • 5 **sunny** [ˈsʌni] sonnig • 5 **windy** [ˈwɪndi] windig • 6 **to fly a kite** [ˌflaɪ‿ə ˈkaɪt] einen Drachen steigen lassen • 7 **to ride a bike** [ˌraɪd‿ə ˈbaɪk] Fahrrad fahren • 26 **gust of wind** [ˌgʌst‿əv ˈwɪnd] Windstoß

"Ha, ha, ha, this is better than a film!" laughs Gus on the ground. "You always say you want an adventure and now you're having one!"

It's so exciting that everyone – even Lou – can't think about anything else.

Tony is sitting very high up in the tree and his kite is stuck on a small branch near him. This is a big adventure and he is very excited.

'Wow, it's a cherry tree!' he thinks. 'Cool! I'm really hungry …' and he takes a bite out of a big, red cherry.

2 **ground** [graʊnd] Boden • 6 **high up** [haɪ‿ˈʌp] hoch oben • 6 **to be stuck** [bi: ˈstʌk] feststecken • 7 **branch** [brɑ:nʃ] Ast • 9 **cherry** [ˈtʃeri] Kirsche • 10 **to take a bite** [ˌteɪk‿ə ˈbaɪt] abbeißen

Tony looks down. 'Now my friends can see that I'm very brave!' he thinks. "But maybe it's time to go down and tell them all about it!" He takes the kite from its branch and starts to climb down slowly.

Suddenly, he sees a big, black cat. The cat is climbing up the tree in Tony's direction!

'Oh no!' thinks Tony. He hides behind some cherries and keeps very still.

The friends see the cat and are scared. They must help Tony!

"Hey cat! Look here," shouts Ernie. The cat jumps down, but Ernie runs into a hole in the tree.

Now it's Gus's turn. "Hey cat!" he shouts and runs very fast. The cat chases him, but it's too slow. Tony sneaks down the tree and disappears into the hole. Now Gus runs into the hole too. The mice are very quiet. After a while the cat gets bored and walks away.

The mice come out, and everyone talks at the same time.

"Are you OK? How was it high up in the tree?"

"It was so cool up there!" Tony says. "I wasn't worried at all. What an adventure! I can't wait to try again!"

Everyone is happy. Only Lou is sad because of her bike. Her friends haven't got it. Nobody knows where it is.

• • •

After lunch, Tony wants to sit on his metal bench outside, in front of his mouse hole. But the bench is not there!

'That's strange,' he thinks. 'Where is it?' He calls to Lou. "Did you take my bench inside?"

7 **to hide** [haɪd] sich verstecken • 14 **to sneak** [sni:k] schleichen • 15 **to disappear** [ˌdɪsəˈpɪə] verschwinden • 16 **after a while** [ˌɑ:ftə‿ə ˈwaɪl] nach einer Weile • 25 **(metal) bench** [ˌmetəl ˈbentʃ] (Metall)bank

"No," Lou answers, "I haven't."

"But I always leave it here, outside the door."

"Ha! That's why I always tell you to bring it inside!" says Lou.

"This is crazy," says Tony. "First your bike and now my bench … where *are* they?"

"Maybe one of the students took them," says Lou. "This is very bad. What can we do?"

• • •

The next morning, it's sunny again and Tony goes out early. He just wants be alone and practise with his kite – then he can show everyone later how good he is! It's a little windy again, and he works hard and tries again and again to fly his kite higher and higher.

'I'm really good at this!' he thinks and he feels so happy and excited that he jumps up – just as a strong gust of wind blows his kite high into the air – with Tony on the end of it!

This time he's really flying – and he isn't worried today. He *loves* flying like a bird and looking down on the world!

Soon, the kite floats down and Tony is at the top of a tree again. This time it's an apple tree.

'Good,' he thinks. 'Look at all these apples!' And he takes a bite. He sits down and looks at the world below. Everyone is very small from his branch in the tree – and everyone is very busy too.

'Everything is so interesting from up here!' he thinks.

Suddenly, he sees a lot of activity in the school garden. 'What's happening there?' he thinks.

---

7 **took** [tʊk] *hier:* haben genommen • 13 **higher** [ˈhaɪə] höher • 16 **air** [eə] Luft • 18 **to fly** [flaɪ] fliegen • 19 **bird** [bɜːd] Vogel • 20 **to float** [fləʊt] *hier:* segeln

Six or more mice are moving all the furniture out of a mouse hole in another tree. 'That's my friends' house!' he thinks. He knows his friends, Kit and Bill, are on holiday – so, what are all these mice doing? He's sure Kit and Bill don't know about it.

'I have to go down and stop those mice,' he thinks. 'Wow! I have the information, and I can stop a crime!' He feels very important again.

Suddenly, Tony sees a big, black magpie in its nest, and the magpie sees Tony. Now Tony worries: What if the magpie takes Tony and flies away with him?

But after a few minutes, the bird flies away, and Tony looks down at the nest. There is something very shiny in it. He moves a little closer. Is that a bike he can see? Yes, it is! It's *Lou's* bike! And there's more. Is that a metal bench? Yes, it's *Tony's* bench! *And* there's a ring, a pen and a bracelet that probably belong to students or teachers.

'Wow!' thinks Tony. '*Another* crime – and again I'm the only one with all the information!'

'I must get our things from the magpie's nest,' thinks Tony. He can see that the magpie is far away. 'OK, I have time,' he thinks, and he sneaks down to the nest.

"My bench!" he says happily, but of course it's very heavy and he can't take it down the tree with him. Not with Lou's bike *and* his kite!

Tony is very busy as he's thinking about what he can do, so he doesn't notice that another magpie lands on the nest.

"What are you doing?" says the magpie. "You can't just come into our home and take our things!"

1 **furniture** ['fɜːnɪtʃə] Möbel *(pl)* • 7 **crime** [kraɪm] Straftat • 9 **magpie** ['mæɡpaɪ] Elster • 13 **shiny** ['ʃaɪni] glänzend • 14 **a little closer** [ə ˌlɪtl 'kləʊsə] etwas näher heran • 17 **probably** ['prɒbəbli] wahrscheinlich • 24 **heavy** ['hevi] schwer • 27 **to notice** ['nəʊtɪs] bemerken • 27 **to land** [lænd] landen

Tony looks up. He feels very brave now. "And you can't just come and steal *our* things! This is *my* bench and this is my friend Lou's bike! I am not the thief here!"

"Oh dear ..." says the magpie, "I think I know what the problem is. My husband and I love shiny things and he brings me a lot of presents. I don't know where they come from, but now you tell me that they're yours. I believe you. You must take your things down to your house before my husband comes back. He gets very angry sometimes."

"OK, but how can I get down with all my things?"

"That's no problem for Maggie the Magpie! Oh, that's my name. What's yours?" asks Maggie.

"I'm Tony," he answers.

"Well, let me help you, Tony. You sit on my back and I can take the bench and the bike. OK – let's go!"

2 to steal [sti:l] stehlen • **3 thief** [θi:f] Dieb/-in • **5 husband** ['hʌzbənd] Ehemann

'Wow!' thinks Tony. This is better than flying a kite. He is flying on a bird. It's great! Tony doesn't want the adventure to stop, but soon they land in the schoolyard outside his mouse hole. Lou can't believe it – is Tony really flying on the back of a bird?

"This is my new friend Maggie," says Tony. "And look what we've got!" Maggie puts the bike and the bench down. Lou is very happy.

"But how …?" asks Lou.

"It's a long story," says Maggie.

"Hooray! Everything is fine again," Lou says.

"No, wait …" says Tony. "I was up in a big tree again and saw something very bad. Some other mice are taking all of Kit and Bill's furniture. We must stop them!"

"Come on, you two!" says Maggie. "Let's go!"

Lou is very excited. Now *she* is flying too! She understands why Tony loves his kite so much. It's great!

Soon they arrive at Kit and Bill's house. They knock on the door and a mouse answers – she is covered in paint. They go in – and there are more mice covered in paint!

"I saw you!" says Tony. "What are you doing with Kit and Bill's furniture? Do you want to sell it? You can't do that …"

"Calm down!" says one of the mice. "We're planning a *big* surprise for them. Their house is very old, so we are painting it. Aren't the new decorations cool?

Tony and Lou look around. It *is* very nice. "Sorry. My mistake," says Tony. "This isn't a crime. This is a great surprise!"

11 **Hooray!** [hʊ'reɪ] Hurra! • 13 **saw** [sɔ:] *hier:* habe … gesehen • 18 **soon** [su:n] bald • 19 **covered** ['kʌvəd] *hier:* beschmiert • 24 **Calm down!** [kɑ:m 'daʊn] Beruhig dich!

"Can we fly with you again, Maggie?" asks Tony.

"Of course," says the magpie. "But now I have to go back and talk to my husband about your things.

"What a day!" says Tony to Lou. "I really love my new kite. And tomorrow is *another day*! More adventures and more crimes to solve, I'm sure!"

6 **to solve a crime** [ˌsɒlv‿ə ˈkraɪm] einen Fall lösen

I want to be famous!

It's another sunny day and Tony and Lou are ready for another adventure.

"Let's go to the beach," says Tony. "I can fly my kite over the water!"

"Yes," says Lou. "And we can take a picnic too."

They run through the tunnels under Thomas Tallis School and tell all their friends to meet at the apple tree.

"A day at the beach! Cool!" they all shout when they hear Tony and Lou's idea.

Ten minutes later the friends start to walk to their special beach on the Thames. They are taking a lot of things with them. In their bags they have swimming clothes, food for a picnic, balls, games and, of course, Tony's kite.

When they get to the beach, a lot of other mice are already there. They find a good place and take their things out of their bags.

1 to be ready for sth [biː ˈredi fɔː ˌsʌmθɪŋ] für etw. bereit sein • 3 **beach** [biːtʃ] Strand

"Let's swim first!" says Ernie.

"No, I want to eat," says Blossom. "Or we could play ball," says Tony.

"Look," says Lou and points to another mouse. "There's a photographer!" Everyone looks. The photographer is taking photos of two models on the beach.

'Maybe this is my big chance,' thinks Lou. 'I would love to be a model too. Hmm ... But what can I do so that the photographer looks at me?'

"Picnic time!" says Blossom. "I'm *really* hungry!"

The friends sit down and start eating and drinking. There is *a lot* of food!

Lou is thinking. 'The photographer can't see me when I'm sitting with everyone. I must find a better place.'

She takes a big, colourful hat out of her bag and puts it on her head. Then she moves away from the group and sits on a big stone.

"Nice hat, Lou!" says Blossom.

"Don't you want to sit with us?" shouts Gus.

"No, I just want to be quiet for a few minutes," says Lou, and looks out at the river.

'Now the photographer can see me,' she thinks.

Suddenly, three big seagulls fly down to the picnic and take some sandwiches.

"No! Go away! Don't take our food!" the friends shout. They jump up and clap their hands loudly, but it's too late. Now there are no sandwiches for lunch!

Then a tennis ball lands near the mice, and a dog runs after it. He is barking loudly and the seagulls are scared. They fly away ... but one seagull steals Lou's hat from her head as he flies over her!

"*No*, not my hat!" shouts Lou, and she thinks 'Now the photographer won't look at me at all!'

5 photographer [fəˈtɒgrəfə] Fotograf/-in • **6 model** [ˈmɒdl] Fotomodell • **7 chance** [tʃɑːns] Chance • **17 stone** [stəʊn] Stein • **23 seagull** [ˈsiːgʌl] Möve • **33 won't** [wəʊnt] wird nicht

Soon, another group of mice come to the beach, put up a volleyball net and start to play.

"Hey!" one of them shouts at Tony and his friends. "Do you want to play with us?"

"Great idea!" Tony shouts back. "But we're very good at volleyball! Are you sure you want to play with us?"

"We're always the winners!" shout the new mice.

"Let's see about that!" says Blossom.

Lou doesn't want to play. She is very angry about her hat and she decides to stay on her stone. She still hopes the photographer sees her if she is without the others.

"Come and play!" says Tony. "We need your help!"

"No, somebody must look after our things," says Lou. "I can see everything from here!"

The volleyball game starts and the two teams are very good. Tony's team is winning and the game is very loud. Suddenly, the ball flies over and hits Lou. She falls off the stone onto the beach. She isn't hurt, but her clothes are covered in sand.

"Are you OK?" the other mice shout.

"No!" says Lou. This beach day is awful for her.

The friends soon decide that they don't want to play volleyball any more and they think about what else they can do.

"Let's fly my kite!" says Tony. He's very excited about it, but the others aren't.

"I know," says Ernie. "Let's go on the river! We can use that." He points to a sandwich box by the river.

"Great idea!" everyone shouts.

"Lou, are you coming?" Tony asks.

Lou thinks for a moment. The photographer is still on the beach. She'll look good on a boat. "OK," she says.

1 **to put sth up** [ˌpʊt sʌmθɪŋ ˈʌp] etw. aufbauen • 2 **net** [net] Netz • 17 **suddenly** [ˈsʌdənli] plötzlich • 17 **to fall off sth** [ˌfɔːl ˈɒf sʌmθɪŋ] von etw. herunterfallen • 18 **hurt** [hɜːt] verletzt • 19 **covered in sand** [ˌkʌvəd ɪn ˈsænd] mit Sand bedeckt • 32 **She'll** [ʃəl] Sie wird

"I want to go too! Please! Please!" shouts Ernie's little brother Joe. He's very excited.

"Ok! Ok! Just stop jumping around and be quiet!" says Ernie. Joe often gets on his nerves.

The friends go to pick up the sandwich box and take it down to the water. For them it's very heavy!

"Come on, sailors!" shouts Tony. "Let's go!"

A lot of mice on the beach are watching as they get ready. Gus and Ernie hold the boat and the others climb in and sit down. Then, Gus and Ernie jump into the boat too. They all like the boat even more because it smells like cheese!

"One, two, three!" shouts Ernie.

"Let's go!" they all shout.

The boat starts to move slowly out into the river, but there are too many mice on one side, so it turns over!

Now the boat is upside down, the mice are swimming around – and all their things are swimming around too!

"My sunglasses!" shouts Lou.

The mice on the beach can't stop laughing.

The mice in the water work together and are very busy. It isn't easy, but at last they can turn the boat back over again.

Suddenly, they hear "Help! Help!" Lou sees that little Joe is still in the water and is too tired to swim any more. She and Ernie swim out to help him, but Lou gets to him first. The others clap and cheer when she brings him back to the boat.

"Thank you, Lou! You're a star!" Ernie and the others say when Joe is back in the boat. Soon they are all ready to try again.

11 **to smell** [smel] riechen • 16 **side** [saɪd] Seite • 16 **to turn over** [tɜ:n 'əʊvə] umkippen • 17 **upside down** [ˌʌpsaɪd 'daʊn] verkehrt herum • 19 **sunglasses** *(pl)* ['sʌnglɑ:ses] Sonnenbrille • 27 **to cheer** [tʃɪər] jubeln

"One, two, three!" shouts Ernie.

"They're going again!" shout the mice on the beach.

This time they go down the river without any problems and everyone has a good time.

'I *really* don't look like a model now!' thinks Lou. She sees the photographer in the distance. He is finishing his work for today. 'He didn't see me with my special hat and now I don't look very nice any more!' she thinks.

When the boat is back at the beach, Lou helps Joe to get off. Suddenly, the photographer is walking towards her. What a surprise!

"Hello," he says. "I'm Ted. I'm from *Mouse Style Magazine*." "Wow! Hi!" says Lou. She is very excited.

"In my free time, I make funny films and post them on the internet," says Ted. I have some clips of you from today and I think you are very funny! Can I use some of them for one of my films?"

Lou doesn't know what to think. A *funny* film? She wants to be a *serious* model!

"Look," says Ted, and he shows her the clips he has.

6 distance [ˈdɪstəns] Entfernung • **7 didn't see** [ˌdɪdnt ˈsiː] hat nicht gesehen • **10 to get off** [ɡet ˈɒf] aussteigen • **15 clip** [klɪp] Clip

"No, please don't use these clips," says Lou. "I don't want everyone to laugh at me!"

"But the clips are so great!" Ted says. "I also have very nice photos of you. Look! Here you're helping your friend in the water. And in this one you look so good in your hat! I can definitely use these – but please let me use the funny clips too. They're *very* good!"

6 **definitely** ['defɪnətli] auf jeden Fall

Lou thinks for a moment. A film star … funny films … maybe that's not so bad!

"OK, cool," says Lou in the end. "It's one way to be famous. It isn't what I planned, but it's a good start."

All the others clap and cheer.

"Lou, our film star friend! What a great end to our day at the beach."

4 **what I planned** [iː ˈplænd] was ich geplant habe • 4 **start** [stɑːt] Anfang

Exercises

1 A birthday to remember: A poem

Some words are missing in this poem!
Write the correct word from the box in each gap.

kite | friends | mice | nothing | right | make |
cake | know | problem | do | worry | name |
plans | wish | clean | disappointed

Tony wakes up early, that's (1) new,
but today is his birthday and he has a lot to (2)!
He has one big (3) – he really wants a kite,
but Lou gives him a T-shirt, he thinks that isn't (4).

He's (5), but he decides not to let it show.
His friends want to surprise him, they don't want him to (6).
They have so many wonderful plans to (7)
for his surprise party, his (8) and even a cake!

In the mouse hole, Tony is making his own party (9),
but Lou tells him to (10), which he doesn't understand.
She goes to plan his party with the rest of the (11),
but there's one (12) after another, it really isn't nice!

Where can they have the party? It's the wrong kind of (13)!
The (14) 'Tom' is on the kite, now that's a serious mistake!
They don't know what to do, it isn't easy for the (15).
But don't (16), this story has a very happy end!

2 A birthday to remember: Finding solutions

Answer the questions with complete sentences.

1. What is Lou's solution *(Lösung)* for the problem with the kite?
2. Why isn't it easy for Blossom to make a cheesecake for Tony?
3. Where can they celebrate Tony's birthday?

3 Up, up and away: A word puzzle

Which words from the story are missing here?
Read the descriptions and write the words in the spaces.
You need one letter for each space.

1. Tony, Lou, Ernie, Gus and all the others are good F _ _ _ _ _ _
2. Tony can't use his kite without this. W _ _ _
3. Maggie the magpie lives in this. _ _ _ T
4. It isn't good to _ _ _ E something from somebody without asking.
5. When something happens and you're not prepared for it, it can be a S _ _ _ _ _ _ _.
6. Lou likes to go to places by B _ _ _.
7. The mice can sit under these on a warm day. T _ _ _
8. Tony's bench is very H _ _ _ _.
9. This is a kind of pet. C _ _

Write down the letters in the dark spaces. Put the letters in the right order so they spell a word, then complete the sentence below.

Every ____________________ is very exciting for Tony and Lou!

4 Up, up and away: Understanding the story

These questions are about important points in the story. Choose the best answer for each question.

1. Why isn't Lou happy?
   a) Tony only thinks about his kite.
   b) One of the other mice has her bike.
   c) Her bike is missing and the other mice don't know where it is.

2. Why is Tony up in the tree?
   a) He climbs up the tree so he can have an adventure.
   b) The wind blows him up with his kite.
   c) He wants to get his kite back from the cat.

3. Why are so many things missing?
   a) The TTS students take them to make their teachers angry.
   b) Maggie takes them because she loves them.
   c) Maggie gets them as gifts from her husband.

4. How do Tony and Lou get their things back?
   a) Maggie and Tony bring them back together.
   b) Tony finds them and brings them back.
   c) Maggie brings them back to Lou alone.

5. What does Tony *think* the mice are doing at Kit and Bill's house? He thinks …
   a) … they are moving things into Kit and Bill's house.
   b) … they are throwing paint all over to make it look bad.
   c) … they are taking things because they want to sell them.

6. Why are the mice *really* working in Kit and Bill's mouse hole?
   a) They want to do something nice for Kit and Bill.
   b) They want to live in the mouse hole.
   c) They want it to look better because it gets on their nerves.

5 I want to be famous: What happens, and when?

Put the events in the correct order. Number them from 1 to 9.

☐ **A** All of the mice fall into the water.

☐ **B** Lou doesn't think she looks like a model any more.

☐ **C** Lou sees a photographer and wants him to look at her.

☐ **D** A volleyball hits Lou and she falls in the sand.

☐ **E** Tony, Lou and their friends go to the beach.

☐ **F** The photographer wants to use film clips of Lou.

☐ **G** A seagull takes Lou's pretty hat.

☐ **H** Lou saves Joe.

☐ **I** Lou goes in the boat with the other mice.

6 I want to be famous: Who says what?

Who says these things?

1. "But what can I do so that the photographer looks at me?"
2. "I want to go too! Please! Please!"
3. "Thank you, Lou! You're a star!"
4. "I'm from *Mouse Style Magazine*."
5. "It isn't what I planned, but it's a good start."

7 After you read

1. Which of Tony and Lou's adventures do you like best? Why?
2. Which adventure would you like to have, and who with? Talk about it with your partner.

Solutions

Before you read

1 All about adventures

a) 1. at a football game, on a train; 2. at a birthday party, in a museum; 3. at a recording studio, on a boat; 4. on holiday, at a market

b) *Lösungsvorschlag:* I'd like to have an adventure on a bike because on my bike I am free. I can visit my friends and we can go to the park and have fun together. It's healthy and it isn't expensive.

c) *Lösungsvorschlag:* You can go to an ice rink, go to the swimming pool, get a dog, learn a new hobby …

2 Tony and Lou's adventures

a) *Lösungsvorschlag:* I think they feel free / happy / excited / scared. Perhaps the bird is Tony and Lou's friend and they want to fly together.

b) *Lösungsvorschlag:* I would like Tony and Lou to go to the sea on the bird's back. Or they can go and visit all their friends.

Exercises

1 A birthday to remember: A poem

1. nothing; 2. do; 3. wish; 4. right; 5. disappointed; 6. know; 7. make; 8. kite; 9. plans; 10. clean; 11. mice; 12. problem; 13. cake; 14. name; 15. friends; 16. worry

2 A birthday to remember: Finding solutions

1. Lou wants to go to the Art room and change the name 'Tom' to 'Tony'. 2. Blossom needs a special kind of cheese for Tony's cake, and she doesn't know if there is any in the school kitchen. 3. They can celebrate Tony's birthday at Blossom's house.